The Language and Meaning

of Flowers

D1707356

Dear

May you radiate like the fragrance of a flower...

This book is written by the flowers. It is a book that speaks through flowers.

This book will make you bloom! It contains a list of 800 flowers and their beautiful and timeless meanings.

This pocket book will accompany you all the time, in your purse, in your kitchen, on the terrace table, in your phone, tablet, or in your Kindle. You can access the meaning of a flower anytime and everywhere, day or night, at a dating or a wedding, and early in the morning in the fragrant garden.

Bejewel your heart with the language of a flower. Give someone a flower imbued with fragrance and a word from the soul. Adorn your garden of flowers with values and virtues. Let your garden blossom into the garden of love. Let your heart radiate like the fragrance of a flower...

To the everblooming flower
To the everlasting blossom
To the all-pervading fragrance

A

Abelia (*Abelia*) – Devotion

Acacia (*Acacia*) – Concealed love

Acacia, Rose (*Acacia*) – Elegance, Friendship

Acanthus (*Acanthus*) – Arts

Achillea Erba-Rotta (*Achillea*) – Elegance, Friendship

Achimenes, also Magic flowers, Cupid's bower (*Achimenes*) – Rare worth

Acorn, oak – Nordic symbol of Life and Immortality

Adam & Eve Root (*Aplectrum hyemale*) – Love, Happiness

Adder's Tongue (*Ophioglossum*) – Healing

African Violet (*Saintpaulia*) – Protection, Faithfulness

Adonis, or Pheasant's eye (*Adonis*) – Recollection of life's pleasure

Agave (*Agave*) – Abundance

Agrimony (*Agrimonia*) – Gratitude

Ague Root (*Aletris Farinosa*) – Protection

Alkanet (*Alkanna tinctoria*) – Purification

Allamanda (*Allamanda*) – Heavenly

Allspice (*Pimenta*) – Compassion

Almond blossom (*Amygdalus communis*) – Awakening, Hope

Aloe Vera (*Aloe*) – Wisdom

Alyssum, or Sweet Alyssum (*Lobularia maritima*) –
Worth beyond beauty

Amaranth (*Amaranthus*) – Immortality, Unfading love

Amaryllis (*Hippeastrum*) – Splendid beauty

American arborvitae, or Northern White Cedar (*Thuja*) – Immortality, Tree of Life

American cowslip (*Dodecatheon*) – Divine beauty

American elm (*Ulmus americana*) – Patriotism

American linden, or Basswood (*Tilia americana*) –
Matrimony

Amethyst, or Bush Violet (*Browallia*) – Admiration

Anemone (*Anemone*) – Expectation, Soothing, Calm

Angelica (*Angelica*) – Inspiration

Angrec, also Darwin's orchid, Christmas orchid, Star of Bethlehem orchid, and King of the Angraecums (*Angraecum sesquipedale*) – Royalty

Anthurium (*Anthurium*) – Hospitality

Apple blossom (*Malus domestica*) – Good fortune,
Preference

Apricot (*Prunus armeniaca*) – Love

Arbor vitae (*Thuja occidentalis*) – Unchanging friendship

Arbutus (*Arbutus*) – I love only you

Artichoke (*Cynara*) – Tender heart, Hope for a prosperous future

Arum (*Amorphophallus*) – Ardor

Asafetida (*Ferula*) – Purification

Ash (*Fraxinus*) – Prudence, Protection

Asparagus (*Asparagus*) – The Symbol of Fertility, The Symbol of the Goddess of Love

Asparagus fern (*Asparagus aetiopicus*) – Fascination

Aspen (*Populus tremula*) – Overcoming fear, Lamentation

Asphodel (*Asphodelus*) – My regrets follow you to the grave, Regrets beyond the grave

Asphodel, Yellow; or King's Spear (*Asphodeline lutea*) – Regret

Aster (*Aster*) – The Talisman of Love, Patience

Astilbe (*Astilbe*) – Love at first sight, I will still be waiting for you

Auricula (*Primula auricula*) – Painting

Autumn crocus, also Meadow saffron, Naked ladies (*Colchicum autumnale*) – Purity, Innocence

Avens (*Geum*) – Purification

Avocado (*Persea*) – Love and Beauty

Avocado tree (*Persea*) – Spiritual nourishment

Azalea (*Rhododendron*) – Care, Womanhood, Romance

B

Babiana (*Babiana*) – Pleasure

Baby blue eyes (*Nemophila*) – Success

Baby's Breath (*Gypsophila paniculata*) – Everlasting love, Pure of heart

Bachelor's Button (*Centaurea cyanus*) – Blessedness, Hope in love

Balm, or bee balm, horsemint (*Monarda*) – Sympathy, Virtue

Balm of Gilead (*Cedronella triphylla*) – Healing

Balsam, or Touch-me-not (*Impatiens*) – Ardent love, Impatience

Balsam tree (*Impatiens*) – Healing and celebration

Barberry (*Berberis*) – Sharpness, Satire

Bamboo (*Bambuseae*) – Longevity, Wealth, Happiness

Banana (*Musa*) – Fertility, Potency

Banyan (*Ficus*) – Luck, Longevity

Baobab (*Adansonia*) – The Tree of Life

Barley (*Hordeum*) – Healing, Protection

Basil (*Basilicum*) – Best wishes

Bauhinia (*Bauhinia*) – Harmony, Synchronization

Bayberry (*Myrica*) – Instruction

Bay leaf (*Laurus Nobilis*) – Perseverance, Glory

Bedstraw, fragrant (*Galium triflorum*) – Love

Bee Orchid (*Ophrys*) – Hard work, Industry

Beech (*Fagus*) – Prosperity

Beet (*Beta Vulgaris*) – Love

Begonia (*Begonia*) – Beware, Deep thinking

Belladonna (*Atropa*) – Silence

Bellflower (*Campanula*) – Gratitude

Bells of Ireland, also Shell Flower (*Moluccella laevis*) – Good luck

Betony (*Stachys*) – Surprise

Bignonia Capreolata, or Crossvine (*Bignonia*) – Tangerine beauty

Bindweeds (*Convolvulus*) – Humbleness

Birch (*Betula*) – Meekness, Gracefulness

Bird cherry (*Prunus padus*) – Hope

Bird of Paradise, also Crane Flower (*Strelitzia*) – Freedom, Faithfulness

Birthroots (*Trillium*) – Modest beauty

Bittercress (*Cardamine*) – Paternal error

Bittersweet (*Solanum dulcamara*) – Truth, Platonic love

Black Bryony (*Dioscorea*) – Be my support

Black-Eyed Susan (*Rudbeckia*) – Justice

Blackberry (*Rubus*) – Healing, Protection

Black Poplar (*Populus nigra*) – Courage

Blackthorn (*Prunus spinosa*) – Difficulty

Bladdernut Tree (*Staphylea*) – Frivolous amusements

Blazing stars (*Liatris*) – I will try again

Bleeding Heart (*Lamprocapnos spectabilis*) – Undying love

Bloodroot (*Sanguinaria*) – Protective love

Bluebell (*Hyacinthoides non-scripta*) – Gratitude, Humility

Blueberry (*Vaccinium*) – Prayer

Bluets (*Centaurea*) – Contentment

Blue Flag (*Iris Versicolor*) – Money

Blue Mountain Sage (*Salvia Stenophylla*) – Clarity

Blushing Bride (*Serruria florida*) – Glimpse of love

Bodhi Tree, or Sacred Fig (*Ficus Religiosa*) – Awakening, Enlightenment, Wisdom

Boneset (*Eupatorium*) – Regeneration, Strengthening

Bonsai tree – Balance, Simplicity, Harmony

Borage (*Borago*) – Talent, Bravery

Bougainvillea (*Bougainvillea spectabilis*) – Passion

Bouvardia (*Bouvardia*) – Enthusiasm

Bracken (*Pteridium*) – Enchantment, Magic

Bromeliad (*Bromeliaceae*) – Wealth, Success

Broom (*Cytisus*) – Humility, Neatness

Bryony (*Bryonia*) – Prosperity

Bryony, black (*Bryonia*) – Be my support

Buchu (*Agathosma*) – Psychic powers

Buckbean (*Menyanthes*) – Calm repose

Buckthorn (*Rhamnus*) – Wishes

Buckwheat (*Fagopyrum*) – Money

Bugle (*Ajuga*) – Cheers the heart, Health

Bugloss, or Viper's Bugloss (*Echium vulgare*) – Falsehood

Burdock (*Arctium*) – Touch me not

Buttercup (*Ranunculus*) – Radiance, Charming, Riches

Butterfly Orchid (*Platanthera*) – Gaiety

Butterfly Weed (*Asclepias tuberosa*) – Heartache cure

C

Cabbage (*Brassica oleracea*) – Gain

Cactus (*Opuntia*) – Endurance, Warmth

Caladium, also Heart of Jesus (*Caladium*) – Joy, Delight

Caladium leaves (*Caladium*) – Joyousness

Calamus (*Acorus*) – Love

Calathea crocata (*Calathea*) – Eternal flame

California poppy (*Eschscholzia*) – Releases the karma of the past that is still held within the heart

Calla lily, or Arum lily (*Zantedeschia aethiopica*) – Magnificent beauty, Feminine beauty

Calycanthus (*Calycanthus*) – Benevolence

Camellia (*Camellia*) – Loveliness

Camellia, blue (*Camellia*) – You are the flame in my heart

Camellia, Japonica (*Camellia*) – Excellence

Camellia, pink (*Camellia*) – Longing

Camellia, red (*Camellia*) – You are a flame in my heart, Innate warmth, Faithfulness

Camellia, white (*Camellia*) – Loveliness, Gratitude, You are adorable

Camphor tree (*Cinnamomum camphora*) – Health, Divination

Candelabra (*Brunsvigia Orientalis*) – Be surprised

Canary grass (*Phalaris Canariensis*) – Perseverance

Candlenut (*Aleurites Moluccanus*) – Enlightenment

Candytuft (*Iberis*) – Indifference

Canna lily (*Canna*) – Confidence in Heavens

Cape chamomile (*Eriocephalus punctulatus*) – Transition

Cape may (*Coleonema album*) – Cleansing

Caraway (*Carum carvi*) – Protection

Catesby's starwort (*Aster grandiflorus*) – Afterthought

Cardamom (*Elettaria*) – Love

Carnation (*Dianthus caryophyllus*) – Fascination, Devoted love

Carnation, pink (*Dianthus caryophyllus*) – Woman's love, Mother's undying love

Carnation, red (*Dianthus caryophyllus*) – Admiration, Divine love

Carnation, purple (*Dianthus caryophyllus*) – Capriciousness

Carnation, solid color (*Dianthus caryophyllus*) – Yes

Carnation, white (*Dianthus caryophyllus*) – Sweet and lovely, Pure love

Carnation, yellow (*Dianthus caryophyllus*) – Rejection

Carrot (*Daucus*) – Prosperity, abundance, and fertility

Carrot, flower (*Daucus*) – Do not refuse me

Catalpa tree (*Catalpa*) – Beware of the coquette

Catchfly (*Silene*) – Youthful love

Catmint, or Catnip (*Nepeta*) – Affection, Beauty

Cattail (*Typha*) – Peace, Prosperity

Cattleya (*Cattleya*) – Mature charms

Cedar (*Cedrus*) – I live for thee

Cedar leaf (*Cedrus*) – Think of me

Cedar of Lebanon (*Cedrus*) – Incorruptible

Celery (*Apium*) – Mental powers, Lust

Celandine (*Chelidonium*) – Joys to come

Chamomile (*Matricaria recutita*) – Patience

Chaste Tree, also Agnus-castus, Chasteberry, Abraham's Balm (*Vitex*) – Holy & Pure; Symbol of chastity and faithfulness to the divine spirit

Cherry (*Prunus cerasus*) – A time of sweetness, love and harmony

Cherry blossom (*Prunus cerasus*) – Beauty of life, Spiritual beauty

Cherry juice (*Prunus cerasus*) – The feminine aspects of beauty, sexuality and procreation

Cherry Tree (*Prunus cerasus*) – Good education

Chervil (*Anthriscus*) – Sincerity

Chestnut (*Castanea sativa*) – Do me justice

Chickweed (*Stellaria media*) – I cling to thee

Chicory (*Cichorium intybus*) – Frugality

China flower (*Adenandra*) – Refreshment

Chinaberry tree (*Melia azedarach*) – The Tree of Knowledge of Good and Evil in the Garden of Eden, Hope and Strength

Chinese aster (*Callistephus*) – I will think of thee

Chinkerinchee, also Wonder Flower (*Ornithogalum thyrsoides*) – Wonderful

Chives (*Allium*) – Usefulness

Christmas rose, also Hellebore (*Helleborus*) – Beautiful year ahead

Chrysanthemum, or Chrysanths, or Mums (*Chrysanthemum*) – Cheerfulness, You are a wonderful friend

Chrysanthemum, orange (*Chrysanthemum*) – Enthusiasm and passion

Chrysanthemum, rose (*Chrysanthemum*) – In love

Chrysanthemum, white (*Chrysanthemum*) – Truth, Devoted love

Chrysanthemum, yellow (*Chrysanthemum*) – Slighted love

Chrysanthemum, violet (*Chrysanthemum*) – A wish to get well

Cineraria (*Cineraria*) – Always delighted

Cinnamon (*Cinnamon*) – Love, Beauty

Cinquefoil (*Potentilla*) – Beloved child

Citron (*Citrus*) – Natural beauty

Clarkia (*Clarkia*) – The variety of your conversation delights me

Clematis (*Clematis*) – Intellectual, Ingenuity

Clivia, or Bush lily (*Clivia miniata*) – Good fortune

Clover, four-leaf (*Trifolium*) – Will you be mine? In addition, each leaf is believed to represent something: the first is for faith, the second is for hope, the third is for love, and the fourth is for luck.

Clover, purple (*Trifolium*) – Provident

Clover, red (*Trifolium*) – Industry

Clover, white (*Trifolium*) – Think of me, Faith

Cloves (*Syzygium aromaticum*) – Dignity

Cockscomb (*Celosia cristata*) – Unfading love

Coconut tree (*Cocos nucifera*) – Finding the inner treasure

Coleonema, white (*Coleonema album*) – Breath of Heaven

Coltsfoot (*Tussilago*) – Maternal love, Caring

Columbine (*Aquilegia*) – Innocence of Mary, Holy Spirit, Wisdom

Comfrey (*Symphytum officinale*) – Money

Compass flower (*Silphium laciniatum*) – Faith

Copaiba tree (*Copaifera*) – Vitality

Corchorus (*Corchorus*) – Impatience of happiness

Coriander (*Coriandrum sativum*) – Hidden worth

Corn (*Zea mays*) – Riches

Cornelian Cherry Tree (*Cornus mas*) – Durability

Cornflower (*Centaurea cyanus*) – Delicacy, Refinement

Coronilla (*Coronilla*); also: crown vetch – Success to you

Cosmos (*Cosmos bipinnatus*) – Joy in love and life

Costmary (*Tanacetum balsamita*) – Sweetness

Cowslip (*Primula veris*) – Grace, You are my divinity

Cranberry (*Vaccinium*) – Heartache cure

Crane flower (*Strelitzia reginae*) – Regal, Fabulous

Crepe myrtle (*Lagerstroemia*) – Eloquence

Cress (*Lepidium sativum*) – Power, Stability, Reliable

Crimson Polyanthus (*Polyanthus*) – Mystery of the heart

Crocus (*Crocus*) – Cheerfulness

Crown imperial (*Fritillaria*) – Majesty

Cudweed (*Gnaphalium*) – Constant remembrance

Cumin (*Cuminum*) – Fidelity

Currants (*Ribes sanguineum*) – You please me

Cyclamen (*Cyclamen*) – Modesty, Humble hope

Cypress (*Cupressus*) – Death of the ego, Mourning

D

Daffodil (*Narcissus*) – Chivalry, Respect

Dahlia (*Dahlia*) – Forever thine, Dignity and Elegance

Daisy (*Bellis*) – Purity, Loyal love

Daisy, garden (*Bellis*) – I share your feelings

Daisy, gerbera (*Gerbera*) – Cheerfulness

Daisy, michaelmas (*Aster amellus*) – Farewell

Daisy, red (*Bellis*) – Beauty unknown to possessor

Daisy, white (*Bellis*) – Innocence

Daisy, wild (*Bellis*) – I will think of it

Dandelion (*Taraxacum*) – Oracle of Love

Daphne (*Daphne*) – Glory

Daphne odora (*Daphne odora*) – Sweets to the sweet

Date-plum (*Diospyros lotus*) – Resistance

Daylily (*Hemerocallis*) – Mother

Dew plant (*Aptenia*); also: baby sun rose – Serenade

Foxgloves (*Digitalis*) – I'll be with you as soon as I can

Dill (*Anethum*) – Good spirits

Diosma (*Coleonema*) – Simple elegance, Usefulness

Disa (*Disa uniflora*) – Seduction

Dittany (*Dictamnus albus*) – Birth

Docks, or Sorrels (*Rumex*) – Patience, Endurance

Dodder (*Cascuta*) – Baseness

Dogbane, or Indian hemp (*Apocynum*) – Inspiration

Dogwood (*Cornus*) – Durability, Undiminished love

Dragon lily (*Dracaena*) – Inner power

Dragon root (*Arisaema dracontium*) – Ardor

Dune bluebell (*Gladiolus rogersii*) – Grateful

Dwarf sumac, or Winged sumac (*Rhus copallinum*) –
Adoration

E

Edelweiss (*Leontopodium alpinum*) – Noble courage, Devotion

Eglantine (*Rosa eglanteria*) – Poetry, Talent

Elder (*Sambucus*) – Compassion

Elecampane (*Inula helenium*) – Tears

Elm (*Ulmus*) – Dignity

Elim heath (*Erica regia*) – Enticement

Enchanter's nightshade (*Circaea*) – Fascination

Endine (*Endine*) – Frugality

Eryngo (*Eryngium*); also: sea holly – Independence

Eucalyptus (*Eucalyptus*) – Protection

Evening primrose (*Oenothera biennis*) – Sweet memories

Everlasting (*Gnaphalium californicum*) – Never ceasing remembrance

Everlasting Pea (*Lathyrus latifolius*) – Wilt go with me?

Eyebright (*Euphrasia*) – Cheer up

F

Featherhead (*Struthiola argentea*) – Allurement

Fennel (*Foeniculum vulgare*) – Strength, Worthy of praise, Flattery

Fern, general – Fascination, Confidence, Shelter, "Mi casa su casa"

Fern (*Polypodiophyta*) – Sincerity

Fern, maidenhair (*Adiantum capillus-veneris*) – Secret bond of love

Fern, royal (*Osmunda regalis*) – Reverie

Feverfew (*Tanacetum parthenium*) – Warmth, Good health

Fig (*Ficus carica*) – Secret, Longevity

Fir tree (*Abies*) – Elevation

Fire lily (*Cyrtanthus guthrieae*) – Passionate

Flax (*Linum usitatissimum*) – I feel your kindness

Fleur-de-lis (*Lilium*) – Message, Flame

Flower-of-an-hour (*Hibiscus trionum*) – Delicate beauty

Flowering quince (*Chaenomeles*) – Symbol of love, Sincerity

Flowering reed (*Typha*) – Confidence in Heavens

Forget-me-not (*Myosotis*) – True love

Forsythia (*Forsythia*) – Anticipation

Foxglove (*Digitalis purpurea*) – Insincerity, Youth

Frankincense (*Boswellia tree*) – The incense of a faithful heart

Foxtail lilies (*Eremurus*); also: desert candles – Endurance

Frangipani (*Plumeria*) – Protection

Fraxinella (*Dictamnus*) – Fire

Freesia (*Freesia*) – Lasting friendship, Innocence

Fringed gentian (*Gentianopsis*) – Look to heaven

French lilac (*Galega officinalis*); also: goat's rue – Reason

Fuchsia (*Fuchsia*) – Humble love, Frugal

Fuller's teasel (*Dipsacus fullonum*) – Austerity

Furze (*Ulex europaeus*) – Love for all occasions

G

Galax, or Wandplant (*Galax*) – Encouragement

Gardenia (*Gardenia*) – Refinement, Purity

Garlic (*Allium*) – Courage, Strength, Get well, Ward off evil & illness

Garlic, blossom (*Allium*) – Prosperity, Strength, Union

Gentian (*Gentiana*) – Integrity, The Flower of Victory

Gentian, fringed (*Gentiana*) – Intrinsic worth, I look to Heaven

Gentian, closed (*Gentiana*) – Sweet be thy dreams

Gentiana Fritillaria (*Fritillaria*) – Virgin pride

Geranium, (*Pelargonium*) – True friend, Gentility, Peaceful mind

Geranium, apple (*Pelargonium*) – Present preference

Geranium, dark (*Pelargonium*) – Melancholy

Geranium, ivy (*Pelargonium*) – Your hand for next dance

Geranium, lemon (*Pelargonium*) – Unexpected meeting

Geranium, nutmeg (*Pelargonium*) – I expect a meeting

Geranium, oak-leaf (*Pelargonium*) – True friendship

Geranium, pencil-leaf (*Pelargonium*) – Ingenuity

Geranium, rose (*Pelargonium*) – Preference

Geranium, scarlet (*Pelargonium*) – Comforting, Consolation

Geranium, silver leaf (*Pelargonium*) – Recall

Geranium, wild (*Pelargonium*) – Steadfast piety

Gillyflower (*Dianthus*) – Lasting beauty

Ginger (*Zingiber*) – Strength

Gladioli, general (*Gladiolus*) – Strength of character, Never giving up, Generosity

Gladioli, red (*Gladiolus*) – Love and Passion

Gladioli, pink (*Gladiolus*) – Femininity, Motherly love

Gladioli, purple (*Gladiolus*) – Charm, grace and mysteriousness

Gladioli, white (*Gladiolus*) – Innocence and purity

Gladioli, yellow (*Gladiolus*) – Cheerfulness and compassion

Globe amaranth (*Gomphrena*) – Unfading love

Gloxinia (*Gloxinia*) – Love at first sight, Proud spirit

Goldenrod (*Solidago*) – Encouragement

Good-King-Henry (*Blitum*) – Goodness

Gooseberry (*Ribes*) – Anticipation

Goosefoot (*Chnopodium*); also: melde – Goodness

Gorse (*Ulex*) – Endearing affection

Grandiflora (*Rosa*) – High souled

Grape (*Vitis*) – Charity

Grapevine (*Vitis vinifera*) – Abundance, Mirth

Grass (*Poaceae*) – Utility

Greenbriers (*Smilax*) – Loveliness

Guelder rose (*Viburnum opulus*) – Winter

Guernsey lily (*Nerine sarniensis*) – Allusion

H

Harebell (*Campanula rotundifolia*) – Delicate as this flower

Hawkweed (*Hieracium*) – Quicksightedness

Hawthorn (*Crataegus monogyna*) – Hope

Hazel (*Corylus*) – Reconciliation, Reunion

Heath (*Erica*) – Solitude

Heather, lavender (*Calluna vulgaris*) – Admiration

Heather, white (*Calluna vulgaris*) – Protection, Wishes will come true

Helmet flower (*Aconitum napellus*); also: Monkshood – Chivalry

Heliotrope (*Heliotropium*) – Devotion, I Love

Henbane (*Hyoscyamus niger*) – For males to attract love from females

Hibiscus (*Hibiscus*) – Unique and delicate beauty; A true symbol of female energy; A symbol of a perfect wife; Hibiscus flowers are gifted to the women who are worthy enough of their beauty and uniqueness

Hibiscus, white (*Hibiscus*) – Female energy, beauty and purity

Hibiscus, purple (*Hibiscus*) – Mystery, higher class and knowledge

Hibiscus, pink (*Hibiscus*) – Friendship and many kinds of love

Hibiscus, red (*Hibiscus*) – Passion, love and romance

Hibiscus, yellow (*Hibiscus*) – Friendship and family relations

Hoarhound (*Marrubium vulgare*) – Frozen kindness

Hoary stock (*Matthiola incana*) – Promptitude

Holly (*Ilex*) – Foresight, Enchantment

Hollyhock (*Alcea*) – Fruitfulness

Hollyhock, white (*Alcea*) – Female ambition

Honesty (*Lunaria annua*) – Sincerity

Honey-flower (*Melianthus*) – Love sweet and secret

Honeysuckle (*Lonicera*); also: St. Mary's Hand – Bond of Love, Devotion

Honeysuckle, Coral (*Lonicera*) – The color of my fate

Honeysuckle, French (*Hedysarum coronarium*) – Rustic beauty

Honeysuckle, Monthly (*Lonicera*) – I will not answer hastily

Hop (*Hops*) – Injustice

Hornbeam (*Carpinus*) – Ornament

Horse-chestnut (*Aesculus*) – Luxury

Hosta, or Plantain lilies (*Hosta*) – Devotion

House-leek (*Sempervivum*) – Vivacity, Domestic economy

Houstonia (*Houstonia*); also: quaker ladies – Contentment

Huckleberry (*Vaccinium*) – Faith

Humble plant (*Mimosa pudica*) – Humbleness

Hyacinth, blue (*Hyacinthus orientalis*) – Constancy

Hyacinth, purple (*Hyacinthus orientalis*) – Please forgive me

Hyacinth, red (*Hyacinthus orientalis*) – Joy

Hyacinth, white (*Hyacinthus orientalis*) – Loveliness, I'll pray for you

Hyacinth, yellow (*Hyacinthus orientalis*) – Jealousy

Hydrangea (*Hydrangea*) – Gracefulness

Hyssop (*Hyssopus*) – Cleanliness

I

Iceplant, or Sea fig (*Carpobrotus chilensis*) – Eloquence, Your looks freeze me

Iceland moss (*Cetraria*) – Health

Impatiens (*Impatiens*) – Impatience

Iris (*Iris*) – Wisdom, Faith, Valor

Iris, german (*Iris*) – Flame

Iris, yellow (*Iris*) – Passion

Ixia (*Ixia*) – Happiness

Ivy (*Hedera*) – Fidelity, Wedded love

Ivy leaf (*Hedera*) – Friendship

Ivy, sprig of white tendrils (*Hedera*) – Affection

Ivy vine (*Hedera*) – Matrimony, Marriage

J

Jacob's ladder (*Polemonium*) – Come down to me

Jacobinia, also Brazilian Plume Flower (*Justicia carnea*) – The perfection of female loveliness

Japanese Maple (*Acer palmatum*) – Blessings

Japanese Pieris, or Japanese Andromeda (*Pieris japonica*) – Happy thoughts, Happiness through the ages

Jasmine (*Jasminum*) – The gift from God; Purity of the spirit; Symbol of women's kindness, gratitude and delicacy

Jasmine, blue (*Jasminum*) – Honesty and trust

Jasmine, cape (*Jasminum*) – Transient joy

Jasmine, orange (*Jasminum*) – Happiness, passion and love

Jasmine, pink (*Jasminum*) – Romance, love and affection

Jasmine, purple (*Jasminum*) – Royalty and nobility

Jasmine, red (*Jasminum*) – Love and passion

Jasmine, spanish (*Jasminum*) – Sensuality

Jasmine, white (*Jasminum*) – Purity, innocence and virginity

Jasmine, yellow (*Jasminum*) – Grace, Elegance

Jersey lily (*Amaryllis belladonna*) – Splendid beauty

Jerusalem oak goosefoot (*Dysphania botrys*) – Your love is reciprocated

Jonquil (*Narcissus jonquilla*) – Return my affection, Love me

Judas-Tree (*Cercis siliquastrum*) – Tree of Love, Reawakening

Juniper (*Juniperus*) – Perfect loveliness

K

Kakabeak, also Parrot's beak (*Clianthus*) – Self-seeking

Kennedia (*Kennedia*) – Intellectual beauty

Kingcup (*Caltha*) – Riches

Kiwi tree (*Actinidia*) – Blessings of a prosperous future

Knotweeds, or Smartweeds (*Persicaria*) – Restoration

Koekemakranka (*Genthyllis afra*) – Virility

Kooigoed, also Most Fragrant Helichrysum (*Helichrysum odoratissimum*) – Compassion

Kranz aloe, or Candelabra aloe (*Aloe arborescens*) – Evanescent

L

Laburnum (*Laburnum anagyroides*) – Pensive beauty

Lady's mantles (*Alchemilla*) – Magic

Lady's slipper (*Cypripedium*) – Capricious beauty

Lamb's ears (*Stachys byzantina*) – Support

Lantana (*Lantana*) – Rigor

Larch (*Larix decidua*) – Boldness

Larkspur (*Consolida*) – Lightness, Open heart

Larkspur (*Delphinium*) – Heavenly transcendence

Laurel (*Laurus*) – Glory

Laurustinus (*Viburnum tinus*) – Cheerfulness

Lavender (*Lavandula*) – Devotion, Love

Lavender rose (*Lavandula*) – Pure love

Leadwort (*Plumbago*) – Spiritual wishes

Leather leaf fern (*Polypodium*) – Fascination

Lemon (*Citrus limon*) – Zest

Lemon blossom (*Citrus limon*) – Faithful love, Discretion

Lettuce (*Lactuca sativa*) – Cold-hearted

Lichen (*Parmelia*) – Solitude

Lilac (*Syringa*) – Spring and renewal

Lilac, blue (*Syringa*) – Tranquility

Lilac, magenta (*Syringa*) – Love and passion

Lilac, purple (*Syringa*) – First love, Humility

Lilac, white (*Syringa*) – Youth, Innocence and purity

Lily, general (*Lilium*) – Purity of heart, Modesty

Lily, casablanca (*Lilium*) – Celebration

Lily, day (*Lilium*) – Enthusiasm, Chinese emblem for mother

Lily, eucharis (*Lilium*) – Maiden charms

Lily, imperial (*Lilium*) – Majesty

Lily, scarlet (*Lilium*) – High-souled

Lily, stargazer (*Lilium*) – Ambition

Lily, tiger (*Lilium*) – Wealth, Prosperity

Lily, water (*Lilium*) – Eloquence

Lily, white (*Lilium*) – Purity, Virtue, Symbol of the Virgin Mary

Lily, yellow (*Lilium*) – Gratitude

Lily of the Incas, or Peruvian Lily (*Alstroemeria*) – Devotion, Friendship

Lily of the Nile (*Agapanthus*) – Love's letter

Lily of the Valley (*Convallaria majalis*) – Return of happiness, Purity of heart, Tears of the Virgin Mary, Humility

Linden tree, or Lime tree (*Tilia*) – Conjugal love, The intimacy and attraction of lovers

Lion's ear, or Wild dagga (*Leonotis leonurus*) – Euphoria

Liquorice (*Glycyrrhiza glabra*); also: Licorice, Belvidere – I declare against you

Lisianthus (*Eustoma*); also: Prairie gentian, Tulip gentian – Appreciation

Live oak (*Queircus*) – Liberty

Liverwort (*Hepatica*) – Confidence

Lobelia (*Lobelia*); also: Scarlet Lobelia, Cardinal Flower – Distinction, Splendor

Honey locust (*Gleditsia triacanthos*) – Elegance

London pride (*Saxifraga urbium*) – Frivolity

Loosestrife, purple (*Lythrum*) – Forgiveness, Take this flower as a peace-offering

Loosestrife, yellow (*Lythrum*) – Peace

Lotus (*Nelumbo nucifera*) – Purity

Love-in-a-mist (*Nigella damascena*) – Perplexity, Delicacy

Love-lies-bleeding (*Amaranthus caudatus*) – Hopeless but not heartless

Lucerne (*Medicago*); also: alfalfa – Life

Lungwort (*Pulmonaria*) – You are my life

Lupine (*Lupinus*) – Imagination, Always happy

Lychnis (*Lychnis*); also: burning love – Spiritual enthusiasm

M

Madagascar jasmine, also Hawaiian wedding flower, Bridal wreath (*Stephanotis floribunda*) – Happiness in marriage

Madder (*Rubia*) – Calumny

Madwort (*Aurinia saxatilis*) – Tranquility

Magnolia (*Magnolia*) – Dignity, Nobility

Magnolia, Chinese (*Magnolia*) – Love of nature

Magnolia grandiflora, or Southern magnolia (*Magnolia*) – Peerless and proud

Mallow (*Malva*) – Sweetness, Gentleness

Mallow, marsh (*Malva*) – Beneficence

Mallow, syrian (*Malva*) – Persuasion

Mallow, venetian (*Malva*) – Delicate beauty

Manchineel (*Hippomane mancinella*) – Betrayal

Mandrake (*Mandragora*) – Soothing, Rarity

Maple (*Acer*) – Wisdom of Balance

Marigold (*Calendula*) – Passion, Creativity

Marjoram (*Origanum*) – Joy, Happiness

Marsh marigold (*Caltha palustris*) – Wealth

Marshmallow (*Althaea*) – Imbued in love

Marvel of Peru (*Mirabilis jalapa*) – Humbleness

Masterworts (*Astrantia*) – Strength, Courage

Mayflower (*Epigaea repens*) – Welcome, Hospitality

Meadowsweet (*Filipendula ulmaria*) – Courtship and matrimony

Mesembryanthemum (*Mesembryanthemum*) – Idleness

Melissa (*Melissa*) – Fun, Sympathy

Mercury (*Mercurialis*) – Goodness

Mezereon (*Daphne mezereum*) – Love in a snow-wreath, Desire to please

Mignonette (*Reseda odorata*) – Health, Your qualities surpass your charms

Milk Thistle (*Silybum marianum*) – Divine love, Royalty, Emblem of the Virgin Mary

Milk vetch (*Astragalus*) – Comfort, Your presence softens my pain

Milkweed (*Asclepias*) – Let me go, Rebirth

Milkwort (*Polygala vulgaris*) – Hermitage

Mimosa (*Mimosa*) – Sensitiveness

Mint (*Mentha*) – Virtue

Mistletoe (*Viscum*) – I surmount all difficulties, Kiss me

Mock orange (*Pittosporum undulatum*) – Fraternal affections

Moneywort (*Lysimachia nummularia*) – Ever faithful

Moonflower (*Ipomoea alba*) – Dreams of Love

Moonwort (*Lunaria biennis*) – Forgetfulness

Moringa, or Drumstick tree (*Moringa*) – The Tree of Life, Growth and Change; The Tree that Never Dies

Morning glory (*Ipomoea*) – Love, Affection

Moschatel (*Adoxa*) – Weak but winning

Moss (*Bryopsida*) – Maternal love

Mossy saxifrage (*Saxifraga bryoides*) – Affection

Motherwort (*Leonurus*) – Secret love

Mountain-ash, or Service tree (*Sorbus*) – Prudence

Mourning Bride, or Pincushion flower (*Scabiosa atropurpurea*) – Unfortunate attachment

Mountain Laurel (*Kalmia latifolia*) – Perseverance

Mouse-ear chickweed (*Cerastium*) – Simplicity

Mugworts (*Artemisia*) – Dignity, Happiness

Mulberry (*Morus*) – Wisdom

Mullein (*Verbascum*) – Good nature

Mustard (*Brassica*) – Intelligence

Myrrh (*Commiphora*) – Gladness

Myrtle (*Myrtus*) – Love

N

Nandina (*Nandina*); also: heavenly/sacred bamboo –
Warm love

Narcissus (*Narcissus*) – Self-love

Nasturtium (*Tropaeolum majus*) – Patriotism, Heroism

Nettle (*Urtica*) – Unity

Nigell (*Nigella*); also: love in a mist – Delicacy

Night-blooming cereus (*Cereus*); also: princess of the
night, queen of the night, Honolulu queen – Modest
genius

Nightshade (*Solanum*) – Truth

O

Oak (*Quercus*) – Liberty, Hospitality

Oak leaf (*Quercus*) – Bravery

Oats (*Avena sativa*) – Music of the soul

Oleander (*Nerium oleander*) – Beware

Olive (*Olea europaea*) – Peace

Ophrys spider (*Ophrys*) – Dexterity

Orange (*Citrus sinensis*) – Generosity

Orange blossom (*Citrus sinensis*) – Eternal love, Pure love

Orchid, general (*Orchidaceae*) – Refined beauty

Orchid, blue (*Orchidaceae*) – Rarity

Orchid, red (*Orchidaceae*) – Passion and desire

Orchid, pink (*Orchidaceae*) – Grace, joy and femininity

Orchid, white (*Orchidaceae*) – Reverence and humility

Orchid, purple (*Orchidaceae*) – Admiration and respect

Orchid, yellow (*Orchidaceae*) – Friendship, New beginnings

Orchid, orange (*Orchidaceae*) – Enthusiasm and pride

Orchid, green (*Orchidaceae*) – Good fortune and blessings

Oregano (*Origanum vulgare*) – Joy
Oriental Poppy (*Papaver*) – Quiet
Osmunda (*Osmunda*) – Dreams
Osier (*Salix viminalis*) – Frankness
Oxeye daisy (*Leucanthemum vulgare*) – Be patient

P

Palm leaves (*Arecaceae*) – Victory, Success

Pansy (*Viola*) – Merriment, Loyalty

Parsley (*Petroselinum crispum*) – Festivity, Gratitude

Pasque flower (*Pulsatilla*) – You are without pretension

Passion flower (*Passiflora*) – Faith

Patience dock (*Rumex patientia*) – Patience

Pea (*Pisum*) – Appointed meeting

Peace lily (*Spathiphyllum*) – Peace, Purity, Harmony

Peach (*Prunus persica*) – Unequaled charm

Peach blossom (*Prunus persica*) – My heart is thine, Bridal hope

Pear (*Pyrus*) – Affection

Pear blossom (*Pyrus*) – Tenderness

Pennyroyal (*Mentha pulegium*) – Leave, Flee

Peony (*Paeonia*) – Compassion, Happy marriage, Happy life

Peppermint (*Mentha*) – Warm feeling

Periwinkle (*Vinca minor*) – Tender recollections, Sweet memories

Persian silk tree (*Albizia Julibrissin*) – Calm the spirit, Spiritual balance

Persimmon (*Diospyros kaki*) – Beautiful resting place

Petunia (*Petunia*) – Your presence soothes me

Phlox (*Phlox*) – Our hearts are united, United souls

Pincushion (*Leucospermum cordifolium*) – Endurance

Pine (*Pinus*) – Hope, Spiritual energy

Pineapple (*Ananas comosus*) – You are perfect

Pink (*Dianthus plumarius*) – Pure affection

Pink, clove (*Dianthus plumarius*) – Dignity

Pink, double-red (*Dianthus plumarius*) – Pure love

Pink, Indian (*Dianthus plumarius*) – Aversion

Pink, Indian, double (*Dianthus plumarius*) – Lovely

Pink, mountain (*Dianthus plumarius*) – You are aspiring

Pink, red (*Dianthus plumarius*) – Pure love

Pink, variegated (*Dianthus plumarius*) – Refusal

Pink, white (*Dianthus plumarius*) – You are fair

Pink, yellow (*Dianthus plumarius*) – Disdain

Pink, wild (*Dianthus plumarius*) – Dignity

Plane tree (*Platanus*) – Genius

Plum blossom (*Prunus domestica*) – Fidelity, Longevity

Plum tree (*Prunus domestica*) – Keep promise

Plum tree, wild (*Prunus domestica*) – Independence

Plume thistle (*Cirsium*) – Independence

Poinsettia (*Euphorbia pulcherrima*) – Birth of Christ

Polyanthus (*Primula*) – Confidence

Pomegranate (*Punica granatum*) – Symbol of life and fertility

Pomegranate blossom (*Punica granatum*) – Mature elegance

Poplar, black (*Populus nigra*) – Courage

Poplar, white (*Populus alba*) – Time

Poppy (*Papaver*) – Consolation

Poppy, red (*Papaver*) – Pleasure

Poppy, scarlet (*Papaver*) – Fantastic extravagance

Poppy, white (*Papaver*) – Rest, Sleep of the heart

Poppy, yellow (*Papaver*) – Wealth, Success

Potato (*Solanum tuberosum*) – Beneficence

Potato vine (*Solanum jasminoides*) – You are delicious

Prickly pear (*Opuntia*) – Hope and endurance

Primrose (*Primula*) – Childhood, Young love, I can't live without you

Primrose, japanese (*Primula japonica*) – Eternal love

Prince's feather (*Amaranthus hypochondriacus*) – Unfading love

Privet (*Ligustrum*) – Mildness

Pumpkin (*Cucurbita*) – Rebirth and fertility, Harvests and crops

Purple coneflower (*Echinacea purpurea*) – Strength and health

Purple pitcher, or Side-saddle flower (*Sarracenia purpurea*) – Will you pledge me?

Pussy willow (*Salix*) – Motherhood
Pyramidal Orchid (*Anacamptis pyramidalis*) – Refined beauty
Pyxie (*Pyxidanthera*) – Life is sweet

Q

Quaking grass (*Briza*) – Agitation

Queen Anne's lace (*Ammi majus*) – Delicate femininity

Quina (*Cinchona*) – Luck

Quince (*Cydonia oblonga*) – Romance, Partnership, Unity

Quinoa (*Chenopodium*) – Willingness, Inventiveness, Compassion

R

Ragged Robin (*Lychnis flos-cuculi*) – Wit

Ragweed (*Ambrosia*) – Mutual love, Love returned

Raspberry (*Rubus*) – Remorse

Red bay (*Persea borbonia*) – Love's memory

Redbud (*Cercis canadensis*) – A breath of fresh air after a long winter

Red shanks (*Adenostoma sparsifolium*) – Patience

Redwood tree (*Sequoia*) – Foreverness, Ancient wisdom

Reed (*Poales*) – Music

Rest harrow (*Ononis*) – Obstacle

Rhododendron (*Rhododendron*) – Beauty and energy

Rhubarb (*Rheum*) – Advice

Rockrose (*Cistus*) – Favor

Romanesco Broccoli (*Brassica oleracea*); also: Romanesque cauliflower – Infinity

Rose of Sharon (*Hibiscus syriacus*) – Persuasion

Rosemary (*Rosmarinus officinalis*) – Remembrance, Devotion

Rosemary, wild (*Eriocephalus paniculatus*) – Warm emotions

Rue (*Ruta*) – Grace

Rose, (*Rosa*) – Love, Beauty, Passion

Austrian Rose – Thou art all that is lovely

Black Rose – Death of the ego

Boule de Neige Rose – Just for Thee

Bridal Rose – Happy love

Burgundy Rose – Beauty within

Cabbage Rose – Ambassador of Love

Campion Rose – You deserve my love

Carolina Rose – Love can be dangerous

China Rose – Grace

Cinnamon Rose – Without pretension

Coral Rose – Desire

Daily Rose – I aspire to thy smile

Damask Rose – Freshness

Dark Crimson Rose – Mourning

Dog Rose – Pleasure and pain

Faded Rose – Beauty is fleeting

Garland of Roses (Wreath of Roses) – Reward of virtue and beauty

Gloire de Dijon Rose – Messenger of love

Hibiscus Rose – Delicate beauty

Hundred-leaved Rose – Pride

Inermis Rose – Ingratitude

Japanese Rose – Beauty is your sole attraction

John Hopper Rose – Encouragement

La France Rose – Meet me by moonlight

Lavender Rose – Love at first sight

Maiden Blush Rose – If you do love me you will find me out

Marechal Niel Rose – Yours, heart and soul

May Rose – Precocity

Moss Rose – Superior virtue

Moss Rosebud – Confessed love

Multiflora Rose – Grace

Mundi Rose – Variety

Musk Rose – Capricious beauty

Musk Rose (cluster) – Charming

Nephitos Rose – Infatuation

Orange Rose – Fascination

Pale Peach Rose – Modesty, Immortality

Pompon Rose – Gentility

Perpetual Rose – Unfading love

Pink Rose – Perfect happiness, Sweetness

Pink Dark Rose – Thankfulness

Provence Rose – My heart is in flames

Purple Rose – Enchantment

Red Rose – I love you, Respect

Rose Leaf – You may hope

Roses, bouquet of full bloom – Gratitude

Rosebud, red – Pure and lovely

Rosebud, moss – Confessions of love

Rosebud, white – Beauty and youthfulness, A heart innocent of love

Striped Rose – Warmth of heart

Sweetbriar Rose – Sympathy

Tea Rose – Always lovely, I'll remember always

Thornless Rose – Early attachment, Love at first sight

Unique Rose – Call me not beautiful

White and Red Roses Together – Unity

White Rose – I am worthy of you, Eternal love, Purity, Spiritual love

White Rose, dried – Death is preferable to loss of virtue

White Rose, wilted – Transient impression

Wild Rose – Simplicity, Poetry

Wilde rose geranium (*Pelargonium capitum*) – Balance

Yellow Rose – Friendship and Joy; one yellow rose with 11 red ones means love and passion

S

Saffron (*Crocus sativus*) – Beware of excess, Mirth

Sage (*Salvia officinalis*) – Wisdom, Good health and long life

Saint-John's-wort (*Hypericum perforatum*) – Inspiration

Salad burnet (*Sanguisorba minor*) – Cheerful disposition

Salal (*Gaultheria*) – Zest

Sassafras (*Sassafras*) – Foundation, Considered choices

Satin flower (*Clarkia Amoena*) – Sincerity, Fascination

Savory (*Satureja*) – Interest

Saxifrage, or Rockfoils (*Saxifraga*) – Affection, Admiration

Scabious (*Scabiosa*) – Unfortunate love

Scarlet fuchsia (*Graptophyllum excelsum*) – Taste

Scarlet Pimpernel (*Anagallis arvensis*) – Change

Schinus (*Schinus*) – Spiritual enthusiasm

Scotch fir (*Pinus sylvestris*) – Elevation

Sea lavender, also Statice (*Limonium*) – Remembrance

Sequoia tree, giant (*Sequoia giganteum*) – Fulfillment of dreams

Shamrock (*Trifolium dubium*) – Lightheartedness

Shea tree, or Shi tree (*Vitellaria paradoxa*) – Healing for mind, body and spirit

Shepherd's purse (*Capsella bursa-pastoris*) – All I have is yours, I offer you my all

Siberian crab tree blossom (*Malus baccata*) – Deeply interesting

Small bindweed (*Convolvulus arvensis*) – Humility

Snapdragon (*Antirrhinum majus*) – Fascination, Gracious lady

Sneezeweed (*Helenium*) – Tears

Snowball (*Hydrangea arborescens*) – Thoughts of Heaven, Spiritual thoughts

Snowdrop (*Galanthus*) – Consolation and hope

Solomon's-seal (*Polygonatum biflorum*); also: St. Mary's Seal, Lady's seal – Protection, Be my support

Sorrel (*Rumex acetosa*) – Affection, Parental affection

Southernwood, or Lad's love (*Artemisia abrotanum*) – Jesting

Spearmint (*Mentha*) – Warm feelings

Speedwell (*Veronica*) – Female fidelity

Speedwell, spiked (*Veronica spicata*) – Resemblance

Spicebush (*Lindera benzoin*) – Purification, Prosperity

Spider flower (*Cleome hassleriana*) – Elope with me

Spindle tree (*Euonymus*) – Your image is engraved on my heart

Spruce (*Picea*) – Hope in adversity

Spurge (*Euphorbia*) – Persistence

Star jelly (*Tremella nostoc*) – Resolve the riddle

Star of Bethlehem (*Ornithogalum umbellatum*) – Purity, Reconciliation

Star tulip (*Calochortus monophyllus*) – Intuition

Starwort (*Stellaria*) – Welcome

Steeplebushes (*Spiraea*) – Victory

Stonecrop (*Sedum*) – Tranquility

Straw flower, or Golden everlasting (*Xerochrysum bracteatum*) – Agreement, Union

Strawberry (*Fragaria*) – Perfect elegance, Perfect excellence

Strawberry Tree (*Arbutus*) – Esteemed love

Sugarbushes (*Protea*) – Courage

Sumac (*Rhus*) – Splendor

Sundews (*Drosera*) – Dew of the sun

Sunflower (*Helianthus annuus*) – Devotion, Dedicated love

Sweet Basil (*Basilicum*) – Good wishes

Sweet Briar (*Rosa rubiginosa*) – Simplicity

Sweet Pea (*Lathyrus odoratus*) – Departure

Sweet Sultan (*Centaurea moschata*) – Felicity, Happiness

Sweet William (*Dianthus barbatus*) – Gallantry

Sycamore (*Platanus*) – Curiosity

T

Tansy (*Tanacetum*) – Resistance

Tarragon (*Artemisia*) – Unselfishness

Thornapple (*Datura*) – I dreamed of you

Thrift (*Armeria*) – Sympathy

Throatwort, blue (*Trachelium*) – Neglected beauty

Thyme (*Thymus*) – Activity, Courage

Tickseed, or Calliopsis (*Coreopsis*) – Always cheerful

Tiger Flower (*Tigridia*) – May pride befriend thee

Tobacco plant (*Nicotiana*) – Healing, Cleansing

Traveler's joy (*Clematis*) – Rest, Safety

Tree mallows (*Lavatera*) – Sweet mood

Truffle (*Tuber*) – Surprise

Trumpet vine (*Campsis radicans*) – Fame

Tuberose (*Polianthes tuberosa*) – Sensuality

Tulip (*Tulipa*) – True love

Tulip, black (*Tulipa*) – Intense love that lives in suffering

Tulip, purple (*Tulipa*) – Abundance and nobility

Tulip, red (*Tulipa*) – Declaration of love, Sincere and strong love

Tulip, rose (*Tulipa*) – The birth of love, The innocence of feelings

Tulip, variegated (*Tulipa*) – Beautiful eyes

Tulip, white (*Tulipa*) – Love - Extreme, Sincere and Idealistic

Tulip, yellow (*Tulipa*) – Concern for the loved one

Tulip Tree (*Liriodendron tulipifera*) – Rural happiness

Turnip (*Brassica rapa*) – Charity

V

Valerian (*Valeriana*) – Considerate, Accommodating disposition

Velvetleaf, or Indian mallow (*Abutilon*) – Meditation

Venus Flytrap (*Dionaea muscipula*) – Caught at last

Venus Looking-glass (*Triodanis perfoliata*) – Flattery

Verbena (*Verbena*) – Sensibility, Pray for me

Verbena, pink (*Verbena*) – Family union

Vetch (*Vicia*) – I cling to you

Violet (*Viola*) – Faithful, Virtue

Violet, blue (*Viola*) – True, everlasting love

Violet, white (*Viola*) – Modesty

Violet, yellow (*Viola*) – Modest worth

Virgin's bower (*Clematis virginiana*) – Filial love

Virginia spiderwort (*Tradescantia virginiana*) – Momentary happiness

Virginia Stock (*Malcolmia maritima*) – Undying love, Lasting beauty

Viscaria (*Silene viscaria*) – Will you dance with me?

W

Walnut (*Juglans*) – Intellect

Wallflower (*Cheiranthus*) – Fidelity, Friendship

Water lily (*Nymphaea*) – Pure heart

Watermelon (*Citrullus*) – Symbol of Intellect, Work and Welfare

Water willow (*Justicia americana*) – Freedom

Watsonia, or Bugle lily (*Watsonia zeyheri*) – Chastity

Wax flower, or Porcelain-flower (*Hoya*) – Sculpture, Wealth and protection

Wax myrtle (*Myrica cerifera*) – I will enlighten you

Weeping willow (*Salix babylonica*) – Forsaken, Melancholy

Wheat (*Triticum*) – Prosperity

White Monte Casino (*Aster*) – Patience

Wild fennel (*Foeniculum vulgare*) – Refreshing

Wild garlic (*Tulbaghia violacea*) – Wholesome

Wild mint (*Menta longifolia*) – Virtue

Wild orchid (*Orchidaceae*) – You are belle

Wild pansy (*Viola tricolor*); also: heart's ease, heart's delight, tickle-my-fancy, Jack-jump-up-and-kiss-me, come-and-cuddle-me, three faces in a hood, love-in-idleness – Think of me

Wild pansy, Purple (*Viola*) – You occupy my thoughts

Willow herb (*Epilobium*) – Pretension, Grieving

Windflower, or Wood anemone (*Anemone nemorosa*) – Sincerity, Symbol of Love

Winter cherry (*Physalis alkekengi*) – Symbol of protection

Wintergreen (*Chimaphila*) – Harmony

Wisteria (*Wisteria*) – Welcome, Poetry, Enduring love

Witch hazel (*Hamamelis*) – A spell

Wood Sorrel (*Oxalis*) – Joy

Woodruff, sweet (*Galium odoratum*) – Humility

Woolflower (*Celosia*) – Joyous affection, Creativity

X

Xeranthemum (*Xeranthemum*) – Eternity, Immortality

Y

Yarrow (*Achillea millefolium*) – Cure for heart
Yew (*Taxus baccata*) – Sorrow
Yohimbe (*Yohimbe*) – Love
Yucca (*Yucca*) – Transmutation, Purification

Z

Zephyr, also Fairy Lily, Zephyr Lily, Magic Lily, Ata-
masco Lily, Rain Lily (*Zephyranthes*) – Sincerity, Love

Zinnia (*Zinnia*) – Thoughts of missing friends, Goodness

The end

is an endless fragrance...

Made in the USA
Las Vegas, NV
09 October 2022